Listen to the Voice of the Water

Robert Edward Harris

Preface

The inspiration for this book came from my trip to Lebanon in November of 1997. It was then that I truly touched on the richness of my family's Lebanese heritage in a way that has changed my view of life and my view of the world. My mother is an American of Lebanese descent. My Great Grandmother came to America in 1896 and my Grandparents came to America in 1911. This book tells a story of love for God, love for mankind and romantic love. It attempts, in sometimes-subtle ways to evoke our deepest feelings, and, in contrast, sometimes it attempts this directly. An unwritten heroine's spirit threads her way through most of the romantic poetry in a hidden story line and she ultimately prevails in "The Groom's Prayer."

The first poem—"Listen to the Voice of the Water"—honors my ancestors in Lebanon. For a long time I have felt a growing sense of personal obligation to honor my ancestors and I became more keenly aware of this need in Lebanon. Thus, "...Listen to The Voice of the Water it is calling your name, Listen to the Voice of the Water it is calling you home."

A few poems touch on the lighter side such as "What is a Periwinkle?" and "The Horse Jumped Over the Moon." They soften the intensity of the strong emotions poured into the other poems.

The first three poems are; "Listen to the Voice of the Water"(1997), "Robert's Love"(1998), and "Captain"(1987), which was written as a tribute to my brother in law, Tom Mushet, who was a victim of cancer. Beginning with "Reaching", which is the fourth poem, all of the remaining poems in this book were written during 1999 and are presented in the order in which they were written.

It is with gratitude and the utmost respect that I acknowledge my mother's cousin Ms. Manell Brice. Without her assistance in copy-editing, this book could not have reached its conclusion. Also I must thank, her sisters Mrs. Helen Johnson and Sister Thomas Marie Brice O.S.B., who assisted in reading my poems and giving feedback throughout the year as this book was coming together. It was Julia Joseph's crayon drawing that inspired "The Horse Jumped over the Moon." And a special mention of my three-year-old niece Morgan Elizabeth Harris who, after a reading of "The Horse Jumped over the Moon," finally agreed that it <u>was</u> the horse.

Last, but most of all, I would like to thank my dear friend Carole Strader who listened patiently to all of my poems, even the many which did not make it into this book. When I would have a dry spell, all I had to do was call my friend Carole and she would give me fodder to work with. Even as I write these few lines, Carole is fighting cancer. As a tribute to her bravery and her compassion for mankind, a portion of the proceeds of this book will be contributed to the fight against cancer. Her faith in God and her eternal optimism, I believe, will result in the successful treatment of her condition. God blesses her and all those who face challenges with their health.

For the persecuted throughout the world, let us all do our part no matter how seemingly small. For the romantic—follow your hearts.

Robert Edward Harris
October 2, 1999

Dedication

This book is dedicated to my mother, Marian F. C. Harris who was kind enough to pass on her Lebanese heritage to my four brothers, three sisters and me. When my mother first read the title poem she said, "'Listen to the Voice of the Water' sounds like something that the American Indians would say." To which I replied, "Well I had to go all the way to Lebanon to hear that expression." Interestingly, she was reading a book of poetry while she was expecting me and decided to name me after the author, Robert Harris.

Table of Contents

Listen To the Voice of the Water

Listen To the Voice of the Water

Listen to the Voice of the Water it is calling your name.
Listen to the Voice of the Water it is calling you home.
In Qadischa, all your prayers will be answered.
In Qadischa, all your dreams will come true.

In Qadischa, the question need not be asked;
It is already known.
In Qadischa the answer will not be spoken;
It is in the voice of the water.

This is the land my ancestors left not so very long ago.
I came to pay them homage and now they are calling me home.
I hear the voice of the water it is calling my name.
I hear the voice of the water it is calling me home.

It is said that the hand of God formed this holy valley.
It is true that here you are closer to our Lord.
This valley is near to Him for those who do His work.
Come to the valley it is calling you home.

Listen to the Voice of the Water it is calling your name.
Listen to the Voice of the Water it is calling you home.
In Qadischa, all your prayers will be answered.
In Qadischa, all your dreams will come true.

©Robert Edward Harris
November 21, 1997

Robert's Love

Robert's Love

If God touched your soul, would it not be so that
he touched your heart?
For is not the heart part of the body and is not the
body part of the soul?
If you were to journey with me only for a moment
in our hearts with our souls
Then would you have a smile or do you in fact
have a smile that is showing itself
Even now for the mere thought, the anticipation
of what might be said next?
Of what might happen next? At last the amore in
me has returned
And all that has held me bound for so long has
disappeared.
For so long bound by some thoughts and running
from fears
This need not be dwelt upon any longer nor will I
for now I have you
And you have captured my imagination endlessly

©Robert Edward Harris
July 4, 1998

Captain

Captain

How many times more must the wind
Be taken from my sails?
Leaving me alone in these waters again…
…As if I had no place to go.
Once again facing the slower gentle breezes,
Which do bring a smile to my face,
But only a smile.
The gentle breezes, which cause the waves
To lap lightly along the port side
Of my ship.
And occasionally spill over the gunnels
Causing feelings of thrill and fear
And hope.
That moment of anticipation is sadly followed
By damp mist that falls from the sky,
As if it were rain.

When I'm here in these waters alone…
Alone after that moment-especially that moment,

A cold chill makes me shivery and makes me
Think of other times that were the same.

And these, these are the times that I hate
To remember when I'm alone in these waters.

8

©Robert Edward Harris
November 5, 1987

Reaching

Reaching

And so we think of the winter passing,
And of the spring soon to come.
Our imaginations fill with never ending
Possibilities of hope, of growth, of change
And excitement that causes us to feel alive within.

…Alive in our hearts, alive in our souls, alive in
our minds.
Reaching further and further for that
Ever elusive happiness that is so seemingly
Closer, so seemingly nearer, than we ever
thought possible.

It is there at our fingertips awaiting our common
reply.
Only to say that, sometimes, it is fair to embrace
without
Knowing what we're reaching for or clinging to
or letting go of.
The answer lies not in the asking, but in the
doing.

*For in reaching to the spring we place in our past
the winter
Which held us so helplessly bound by our own
disenchantment.
And now we have the season upon us which
allows us more
In thought, more in doing, and more in fulfilling
our dreams.*

*For spring is here now. Reaching, not asking,
reaching to pull
Us towards that simple smile that should be upon
our face
Always, as it certainly is now. So the spring
reaches,
But do we dare to reach back? Do we dare to try?*

*Robert Edward Harris
February 14, 1999*

Robert Edward Harris

Painted Faces

Painted Faces

Still not old enough to know
What I'm looking for
But I do know
That we paint our faces
And we become someone
Or something else
And the world looks
While we watch

And if they smile, we go on
With our painted face
Or we change and we
Paint a new face
She does
And I do
Until we paint on canvas

We paint our faces,
We wash them off
Someday… only to start
All over again

> *But I'm still too young to know*
> *What will please you*
> *I'm not sure who you are*
> *Or who I am*
> *But I'll keep painting*
> *That's all I want for now.*

> *©Robert Edward Harris*
> *March 5, 1999*

15

The Key to Life

The Key to Life

The Key to life is playing
The hand that has been dealt
With grace and dignity
The key to life is to never give up
Never to quit, never to stop trying
Never to compromise your values
For that is what clearly defines
Who you are and that is all we have
I wish you well in all that you do
And know that we will see each other
In God's house.

©Robert Edward Harris
March 9, 1999

17

A Book Is Missing

A Book Is Missing

Read all that I can and
Listen as closely as I shall
But through it all it is known
That a book is missing

Where shall I learn what I must know?
So as to do the things that must be done
For a book is missing and I know not why
I can not find this word

It has not all that I need to know
But it is as a scroll missing, gone
And where will I look for what I need?

It is not in a book or a scroll but it is in my heart
And so I will not read nor will I search
For all that I need is here and it always has been

A book is missing, perhaps.
But my heart is here and it is right with my God
So I go on without this knowledge
For it will not be missed nor needed
For the truth is that life is simple
And it is I who have made it complex.

There is no book missing, all is complete-all is
finished
And now I must move on for my reading is done
I have learned all that is needed for now
The rest will come to me as it always has
There is no book missing.
There never was.

©Robert Edward Harris
March 9, 1999

20

The Gardener

The Gardener

Is it the beauty of the flowers in the garden?
Or the smell of the lilac in the air
A sunny afternoon after a rain has renewed
So much by giving life a chance to carry on

Of these things and more, which have I missed
today?
Which have I forgotten from my youth?
Which will I forget in my aging and
Why do we question the beauty in the garden?

For I have not come to walk in a small plot
Filled with flowers overhead that lock me in
My time is not here so why must I search
Why must I look in a garden so limited?

There is a greater joy in walking with you.
Take me from this meadow which is so confined
And into your house where I might see
The beauty of so much that will set me free

We implore you to come upon our journey
Shamefully though we must admit
That it is we who should be summoned on
To take our journey with thee

If we toil so much when we shouldn't
And we toil so little when we should
How worthy not are we to ask
That you would allow us in

For your garden oh Lord is large and great
And not one of us would want for more
Than the beauty you share with us at the time
That you walk with us and finally we are there

©Robert Edward Harris
April 5, 1999

23

Lost In A Dream

Lost In A Dream

To be lost in a dream we need only to allow
Our imaginations to carry us to where we know
we should be.
Time will not wait for us-we must enter that
world.
And so we go into that place, that land so far
away
But yet so near -so close to our hearts.

For to be there is not a dream-it is a hope.
It is a longing to be home and not lost in a dream.

The dream starts when we are young and builds
little by little.
No one else knows and no one else believes nor
could they
For I am lost in a dream and no one else believes.
For though I tell them they cannot understand.

So I dream my dream, I search for my path
And I travel alone lost in a dream.

To let others see part of this vision is unfair.
For only he who holds the key may have this
dream.

This is my calling to be lost in a dream.
A dream sent to me from afar and now a dream
coming true.
A dream unfolding even before the eyes of those
whom could not see.
A dream no longer leading me but a dream, at
last finding me too.

©Robert Edward Harris
April 9, 1999

Time Is the Key

Time Is the Key

*Until I hear from you again the eagle will not
soar.
Until I see your smile within, my raiment will be
dull.
This is clearly a reflection of a heart that has
grown cold.
For though thousands gather about, I am alone
without you.*

*Waiver just a little and perhaps you will find,
That another has summoned himself to do the
same.
In that happening could be the coming of a day I
pray,
When your smile within is seen again.*

*Listen to my words for I am calling.
Listen to your heart and you will find
The only thing that keeps us apart is a slight
hesitation.
Oh how terrible a thing so little can be.
What was meaningless has taken on new
importance,
For what it has caused not to happen.*

Drown yourself not in sorrow, but rather
I pray you to open yourself with complete
abandon
To the quickened pace that your heart desires.
For I am waiting and my raiment is black.

Too young they say, too young for this.
For since I have seen your smile no other will do.
And you have not reached to me as I have to you.
Though I must believe that in your heart you are
reaching too.

Time moves on and my heart is as a pendulum
swinging.
The time is now; the key is in your heart,
And the door is waiting at my brow.
For I know what is on the other side.
The key you must send to me, opening up
The treasures we will carry together.

*You left me standing with a thought that was not
finished.
You left me standing with a body that had not
movement.
You left me standing and now I wonder-if only
time was needed.
Only to ask why I have taken so long and why
you have been so patient.
A pause can be so cruel.*

*Time is the key and now I have found
That always with me was the answer.
The question too is easy, for knowing your
thoughts
Guides me closer as I find a door never locked,
but simply waiting.*

*Robert E. Harris
April 27, 1999*

Fear Conquered

Fear Conquered

To calm myself with written word
As if to pour my soul upon
A mirror closely hanging to the thoughts
Coming from my feathered quill.

Is this for the world to see?
Or have I something to be seen
By eyes-only that belong to thee.
Or better still by eyes-only that belong to me.

Talking I have found, to myself again
But will not tell a soul we agree.
In the end only you will know
For a mirror cannot talk, this I can see.

In listening you do so well.
Patience you have for as long as I need.
No other could ever equal
The attention you have shown to me.

No sudden joy will be found
In understanding what you mean.
If you do not share with the world
All that you and I have seen.

I will let you rest for now my friend
But I will return soon you know.
To reflect upon these thoughts we share
And to find where next we should go.

Robert E. Harris
April 28, 1999

33

What is A Periwinkle?

What is A Periwinkle?

On the lighter side they say.
Could I write of fun and play?
I will search my thoughts to see
Answers for questions such as these.

For What is a periwinkle? A flower surely not.
Perhaps a weed growing in a pot.
What silliness has caused me to think,
That an unwanted flower could grow in an old
sink.

In a junkyard without a dog,
Next to natural stones along-side a log
But a periwinkle is not as natural as you think.
We are really not sure what it is or why it's in
that old sink.

Someday soon we will figure it out.
I hope it's before the summer drought.
Now that we have had this bit of fun
At last we can get back to what needs to be done.

Sooner or later a flower goes to seed.
This is something that a flower does need.
If you come back next year and look in that old
sink.
You will find once again the confounded
periwink.

Although research has been scant
The periwinkle is no ordinary plant.
For though there are no ties to the ancient Incas
The periwinkle has roots reaching the vincas

Robert Edward Harris
May 21, 1999.

Robert Edward Harris

Victory and Freedom

Victory and Freedom

The walls are down
None to hold me in
At last I have found
A place to begin

The world still waiting
Patiently to see
When they come down
Where I will be

But the walls are down
And I have discovered
Under the ground
A treasure uncovered

History has shown
We long to go back
To what was known
Before the attack

The walls are down
At last I am free
For I have found
The treasure for me

Build them up higher
To keep danger out
What of our desire
Lost in the drought

The walls have come down
And I am now breathing
Hearing new sounds
Like a child teething

Simply lost was I
Who has taken so long
To see the open sky
This cannot be wrong

For the walls have come down
No need for caution
I will pick up the crown
And accept this option

The walls have come down
And you do know
Many years of freedom
Take years to grow

It was not I who started
What has led to this
But it was I who parted
Without a kiss

Return I must
For it is written
Return unto dust
Where all is forgiven

It will not be soon
So much to be done
But I have the room
And have now begun

For the walls are down
This you must know
And at last I have found
Where I must go

©Robert Edward Harris
June 17, 1999

One of Six

One of Six

Someone has been speaking
Of a moment fleeting
When two people meet
And the friendship is complete

Friends from the start
Without even trying
Though happiness might part
And there could be crying

But the friendship never ends
If it is one of the six
For resolve always mends
If it needs to be fixed

Not to limit friendship's meaning
For we thought we knew
But it would be demeaning
If we expected a slew

Room for more than two
Not enough for ten
A compromise will do
Divide by two add a friend

In case you thought I've finished
I have one thing left to do
To tell a certain person
That one of the six is you

©Robert Edward Harris
June 23, 1999

43

The Groom's Prayer

The Groom's Prayer

My love, where is your hand?
For the dawn comes only once each day,
And to ageless skies a difference does not make.
Seasons come, seasons go,
But my love for you fades not-it grows.
No longer can I bear to wait
For you to become my bride.

Now the time has come at last
For me to properly ask
For your hand from those who give.
In times before, you could not feel
My heart telling of my love,
Nor understand my hidden fears

I have conquered all that has held me back
And seek forgiveness for taking so long
But I am just a man as I have said
And the fear that ran through my veins
Is now completely gone,
For my love for you has prevailed

My pen cannot flow with feelings
Nor my paper know words written
My fear has changed this day
Aching for your answer
I know how lonely it does feel
When true love leaves you waiting
For only one answer will do.

What have I done to take so long?
Forgiveness from you I pray will come
When soon we do become as one
And promises all I will keep.
For you hold my heart as ransom-
A clever one you are,
To have done what no other could do-
All that I have guarded carefully,
I give freely to you.

My heart you have captured,
I have told you this before.
And nothing is held back,
For even my soul you now have
And in years to come you will find
That I will love you more and more

Love like this is not fleeting
But the chance could pass us by
So open up your heart
And take this silver platter-
All you have been waiting for
Is now about to happen

God has blessed us more greatly
Than we ever could have imagined,
Leading you into my arms
And leading me back to you.
I see our future every night
And give Him my gratitude

Confessing to God our hopes and fears,
Knowing all has been forgiven.
And like the promise of His love
Our love will keep on giving
Let us rest more easily
With this new beginning

Take comfort for at last you know,
What has stirred my feelings.
This story I have told only to you
And have given away all else.
For my chance to be in your heart,
I would trade the world

If my question goes unanswered,
How saddened I will be
For only "yes" can bear the fruits
Of what the future can give
"Where is your hand?" need not be asked
For the answer is already known
Till the end of time we will be together
Together we will meet Him at His throne

©Robert Edward Harris
June 24, 1999

Listen Gently

Listen Gently

Listen gently for praises
I was singing to my Lord
And while I stopped to listen
Gently this response played to me

A chorus of two I must say gently
The Lord sent a bird to my door today
Outside waiting music for to play
Melodies so beautiful tears did fall

Then the music was too soft
Gently fading not the music but I
Tired am I spirit pleading gently
For one more round of music

Then a bird returned louder still
And with it was another voice
Chorus of two as I have said
The music divinely inspired

No longer is the spirit drifting
Uplifted from all and ready again
The spirit arose in triumph to say
The voice of God I will obey

©Robert Edward Harris
June 28, 1999

Second Chance

Second Chance

Listen not to your lullaby
For a child no longer am I
From this point onward I choose
Songs dancing from the sky

When lightening strikes near
My feet on solid ground
Gone are my greatest fears
Comfort's spirit I have found

World closing fast within
When most are opening up
Allowing me to focus in
On He who gave the cup

Enter on, exit, some spin about
What are we all here for?
The choice is yours no doubt
To go quietly or to do more

Words unspoken travel not far
Of this I am now certain
As some new poetic star
Awaits the open curtain

©Robert Edward Harris
July 1, 1999

54

In God's Time

In God's Time

Write a song for whom to sing
Or a poem with no-one to listen
And I cannot touch you
Are you still there?

Why do you not answer me?
My pros have disappeared
So I ask you again,
Are you still there?

It consumes me night and day
Knowing that you have captured me
Without you I will be empty forever
Are you still there?

Soon the waiting will be over
And I will see you again
Are you still there?
Or have you chosen a new venue?

I ask so coyly because of my fear,
Since I do not know the answer.
Did you think I would ask?
An answer is a courtesy I prefer.

I am resting but am not rested
I am thinking but have no thoughts
I am hoping but know only despair
Are you still there?

It is so fitting
That I write this note
On scraps of paper blue
For I am finished without you

Soon the time will be upon us
As will the answer to all my questions
But I am so afraid to know
If it is that you are no longer there.

I have been clinging to you
You were right-the feeling has not faded
For though I cannot touch you
I yearn for you day after day, even for years.

How I love you and I always will
I pray that you will still be there
If you knew my longing for you
You would be waiting even now

If you could only feel
How heavy my heart is
If you could know for one day
How deep my longing goes

Your tears would fill the oceans
But that is not what I want
I want your smile and your happiness
Are you still there?

©Robert Edward Harris
August 3, 1999

Robert Edward Harris

58

Battle of the Hearts

Battle of the Hearts

What am I to do?
Pull a star from the sky?
Or should I wave a flag
Above my head as the victors do?

Or wave a flag above my head
As the victims do?
And in my surrender do I win?
Either way I am waving at you.

You do not care if I am the victor
For I still would not capture you.
You care even less if I surrender
As you want not for prisoners.

What does it matter?
For the sky would not miss one star.
Yet I know not how may stars I should gather
To gain your favor.

I can pull a star from the sky
This I have done before.
But never before have I waved a flag or head
As captive, victor over anything more.

In winning and in losing
I am doing all that I can.
Either way though you seem
To be drifting-this I do not understand.

You are my prisoner
But you laugh and jeer.
You are my captor
But you fail to steer.

Oh sure, I have pulled stars from the sky
And I am leaning on one now.
Yet you have not noticed
Perhaps that's why I cannot surrender.

The answer now has come to me
It is not because I do not want to.
The reason is quite simple dear
It is because I do not know how.

It is not that I always get what I want,
I need not explain this to you.
It just that it seems unfair,
Unless of course-you are unsettled too.

Maybe I cannot draw a conclusion
When there is none to be made
Although given time perhaps
This confusion will fade.

Why do I write of a battle
When it is our hearts I am thinking of?
This should not be so difficult
If it is true love.

©Robert Edward Harris
August 15, 1999

Living Water

Living Water

To the water's edge for a cool drink
In the last of these hot summer days
Yet time allows you not what is before you
You turn to what should be lost

Why not to what is needed?
You are so close yet you turn-you need time
The time will not come to you—it is not alive
The past will not run to you-it lies sleeping

Your mission has been given
Yet you flounder fanning direction
So travel then to where they wait
Where they will hear and rejoice

The world has its challenge waiting for you
Nothing inhibits you-nothing is holding you back
Go and seek your peace- the world is waiting
Run to it faster than ever before-run to it

Worthy is the challenge and ever more divine
When victory shares the cool drink at water's
edge
Alone you will not longer be
When nations quench their thirst at summer's
end

Robert Edward Harris
September 7, 2000

The Horse Jumped over the Moon

The Horse Jumped over the Moon

The horse jumped over the moon tonight
For how could it have been the cow?
You don't know much about farms I see
So I'm going to teach you now.

You know things aren't always what they seem
Like the story of the chicken and the egg
And the pig in the mud isn't as happy as you think
In the morning when breakfast is made.

A duck doesn't always land on the pond
Sometimes he's not sure what will pop up
Like the turtle that's lurking underneath
Waiting to eat him up

And the horse jumped over the moon tonight
Please stop telling people it was the cow
And I won't tell that your mind's in flight
As I tricked you into thinking like a child

I guess I've milked this for all that I could
Unless you're laughing now
Because the joke's on you once again
You see it really was the cow.

Well a horse can jump
And a tree leaves a stump
But there's one thing I can't figure out
Something jumped over the moon tonight
But how could it have been the cow?

As the tree that has gone before its time
Once again I've left you stumped
For in the end as in the beginning
I still believe it was the horse that jumped.

Robert Edward Harris
September 10, 1999

68

A Book Is Written

A Book Is Written

Sorry I must go so soon father
Can you not hear what I have heard?
My poetry calls me and is calling me even now.

Not those poems which paper has found
But the few more that paper has not known
Run I must to paper and pen
To speak a little with my long lost friend
For away she has been and now has returned
Just as a gift from God is simply given, not
earned

Your pardon I do eternally beg
But to my gift I have been enslaved
To write of things known only to me
And share them so that I might be freed

But freed from what you might be asking
It is these thoughts that have been so tasking
In a few words I could not share
So I am writing a book for my thoughts to bare

This page in a moment you will read
But the book will take longer it is true
For convincing a world to take heed
To ask of one poem is simply unfair

A book is written one page at a time
We put them together in order to bind
A story that could easily go untold
But regrets then would unfold

If I told you the truth you would not believe
So I tell you nothing and you understand
But tell I must even If I lose all
For denying the truth was the beginning of mans
fall

A book is written one page at a time
The one, which is missing soon to be found
So then when finished and pen put down
At last a bit of rest will be found.

©Robert Edward Harris
September 12, 1999

Marathon

Robert Edward Harris

Marathon

Just as a runner laces his shoes
One last time before the start
I too prepare to begin
And look to find my part

Searching for what I already know
Somehow seems useless to me
So I offer to you this casual glance
As I pass the viewing stands

It was not I who chose this course
But it is I who must finish the run
For I am but a messenger
Still holding the baton

In old England the price would be
Nearly twice as much
And where else could you find
Such a victor for half a crown

Running to win and so soon
You will know what I'm speaking of
World throughout is certain though
Half of anything is not enough

Medals have adorned my neck
But none like that of my heart
I tell you that I'm ready now
And that should be enough

Do not rethread the eye
Nor spend time on trivial things
For this athlete's ready to run
And home awaits his destiny

Worry not about the finish
Once the race has begun
For as my trainer has said
The race is already won

Not for you to take a chance
For it is the runner who must
Again I give you a glance
As we build upon our trust

You will see more clearly
As we round the next turn
A book is for more than reading
For this race is to be won

__But no one will be reading__
__Of what I have not done__
__So I offer these words to you__
__In return for the race I'll run__

__©Robert Edward Harris__
__September 13, 1999__

75

A Box of Wishes and Feelings

A Box of Wishes and Feelings

That box of wishes and feelings
That so tightly conceals
Hopes and dreams you're hiding from
For fear that they can't be real

But dreams do come true
And what more is a wish
Than a moment's hope
For a dream to unfold

And Feelings surely are to be shared
For to hide them is not fair
How will we know what you're thinking of?
Are you hiding away your thoughts of love?

Should you open up to let others in
I think you will find again and again
That wishes and feelings must be shared
And every princess is a little scared.

So chase away your fears today
For a box collector has come to say
Your wishes and feelings must be shared
I have never met a box that cared

For a collector knows what a box can mean
It gives us a way to easily retrieve
But now is your time to figure out
A box can't hold feelings that want out.

©Robert Edward Harris
September 23, 1999

Oliver

Oliver

In a certain light you did teach us that in life,
There is no black and white, only shades of gray.
Gentle and faithful our constant companion
Reminding us again and again until we
understand.

Oliver, where are you now?
Can you see they are killing Christians?
They want to be free.
Timor now, but others before and after.

They were killing Christians in Kosovo
But what a bloody pond was made
When in revenge, thousands
Thousands of Muslims lay dead.

They see no gray, Oliver, black and white only
As the innocent are feeling so lonely
God is listening but bloodshed persists
As he gives us the chance to resolve this mess

We should not avenge what happens
Yet over and over in this world of doubt
They claim each other's lives for vengeance
Until senseless becomes a fitting word.

Let us run today, Oliver, and chase away our
tears
Our hearts are bleeding and nobody cares
Run faster and further to stop our thinking
Of a world in ruin—who will stop the bleeding?

Distance behind us so much further to run
Let us forget about these things and continue on
The miles to come will ease our sorrow
Even though we must return before tomorrow.

They cannot hear, Oliver, they cannot hear
But you understand and have made it quite clear
For black and white adorn your back
And bring to us a smile when we're on the track.

You are the one who showed us in that certain
light
There is no need for such senseless fights
For a shade of gray in the morning predominates
And the black and white is now made one.

Always differences do remain
As generations work through their pain
Let them listen, Oliver, to what you have said
And find a proper way to grieve for the dead

All that we have is this hope
That in a certain light they will see
Shades of gray that you have shown
To those of us who at last are free

Their tears are not falling; they are held in
Yet to turn away is man's greatest sin
And we the guilty comfortably deny
As a world of innocents are sentenced to die.

What can we do—it's a world away?
Yet the treachery comes closer each day.
Tears will fall when it changes our western way.
Will they be looking then for shades of gray?

©Robert Edward Harris
October 1, 1999

Closing Comments

During the month of October 1999 my friend Carole Strader had received the good news that all went well with her cancer surgery. She was told that she had an excellent chance that all of the cancer was removed and this was later confirmed. In that same month we learned that Sister Thomas Marie Brice O.S.B., my mother's cousin and my spiritual mentor, was diagnosed with cancer.

My efforts to have this book published cease. It was unimportant to me at that time as we were focused on Sister in her illness. On January 10,2000 Sister Thomas Marie died. My loss is unexplainable, except perhaps, through my poetry.

The Wind

The Wind

Sister Thomas Marie Brice, O.S.B.

Now the waiting is over
The wind chased us down today
Not to press us for another act to play
But to question our talk of cradle days.

The wind is cold as it hits our faces
Yet in feeling it-it gives a warm embrace
As we are given the time to retrace
Days gone by but telling still

Years in service to do his will
Tears are falling-yours and mine
Her years all left now behind
What a mountain we still have to climb.

She guides us on in subtle ways
One day at a time she reminds us still
To do our best is to do God's will.
We look to the future with courageous faces.

We have known one of God's helpers today
This secret we did keep
Ordinary though she seemed
Living her life to earn her wings.

Changing the world one person at a time
Each time I marveled to see her work
In the end this is what we have
Reflections of one who loved the lord.

The wind is uplifting in its way
Someday coming for each of us
One of God's Angels it now has found
Carrying her gently-heaven bound.

A beautiful kite taken away
No strings left to pull her back.
The wind is cruel yet kind today
For what we have lost, God has found.

Drifting though she never was
As closer to our Lord she drew
The spool finally became undone
And her life as an Angel has now begun.

Robert Edward Harris
January 10, 2000

Robert Edward Harris

Reflections of the Burial of Sister Thomas Marie Brice, O.S.B.

A Song to 'The Sorrowful Mother'

A Song to 'The Sorrowful Mother'

What child is this who lies quietly in your arms?
My sorrow you do know-as on the day they took
your Son
How happy you must be to know that you were
the chosen one
To bring into the world the Lord's only Son

What good comes from this? I must know to
comfort me
Pray for me Mother Mary-again this sinner asks
What child is this who lies quietly in your arms?

The snow is as a blanket on this day they send
her home.
As it was on the day the Lord sent to us your son.
What child is this who lies quietly in your arms?

Your Son was sent to save the world
And this He has done.
She was sent to save a few
Of which I'm certain I am one.

***What child is this who lies quietly under the
snow?
Now at last she is in your arms
And the Lord is happy she is home.
What child is this who lies quietly in your arms?***

***Robert Edward Harris
January 18, 2000***

Epilogue

It was fitting that on the flight to Minnesota for Sister Thomas Marie's funeral at St. Scholastica Monastery that sitting on one side of me was her sister Manell and on my other side was an American Indian tribal member. In our discussions on the flight I discovered in him a genuine sensitivity like none that I have ever seen demonstrated by what had been a complete stranger just minutes earlier. He shared in my sadness as I told him the story of our loss and I was compelled to give him a copy of "The Wind". I had copies with me to take to the Sisters at St. Scholastica. He respectfully held the poem throughout the entire flight taking care to never wrinkle or fold the paper. We bonded in a special way on that day as I was thinking of my mother's words "'Listen to The Voice of The Water' sounds like something the American Indians would say."

Despite all that the American Indians have been through, most of them have chosen to "Listen to The Voice of The Water" and they also learned the lessons of "Oliver". Even though their rightful claims regarding injustices of the

past are overwhelming, they have chosen to be peaceful. They have my respect and my prayers go often to the "Big Chief in the Sky" for them and others who have suffered injustices.

Byblos, Lebanon 1997
©Robert Edward Harris

***A published account of the author's travels in
Lebanon can be found in the April 1998 issue of
the Journal of Maronite Studies (©1998).
www.mari.org/JMS/april98/.***

92

About the Author

Born in the hills of West Virginia, Robert Edward Harris received a degree in economics from Marietta College in Ohio. He then moved on to New York City where he lived for six years while working in the corporate banking business. He relocated to the Washington D. C. area in

1987 and has continued to work in finance as an advisor and as a banker. He has traveled to the Far East, Europe, the Middle East, the Caribbean and throughout most of the U.S.

www.ingramcontent.com/pod-product-compliance
Lightning Source LLC
Chambersburg PA
CBHW031314060726
47590CB00003B/1208